What's in this book

This book belongs to

_____

新年快乐! Happy New Year!

学习内容 Contents

沟通 Communication

拜年
Greet people at Chinese New Year

生词 New words

☆	新年	new year
☆	这里	here
☆	多少	how many, how much
☆	糖果	sweet
☆	问	to ask
☆	给	to give
☆	今年	this year
	去年	last year
	明年	next year
	学	to learn

新年快乐！

Happy New Year!

这里有多少颗糖果？

How many sweets are there?

制作窗花

Make window decorations

中国农历新年

Chinese New Year

Get ready

1 Do you know when Chinese New Year is?

2 What do people do and say for Chinese New Year?

3 Have you ever celebrated Chinese New Year?

xīn nián
新年

"新年快乐，身体健康！"
浩浩和玲玲说。

“这里有多少颗糖果？”
浩浩问玲玲。

gěi
给

"我猜有三十颗，给我一颗。"玲玲说。

"没有三十颗。There are twenty sweets."奶奶说。

"奶奶，您会说英语吗？"
浩浩和玲玲惊喜地问。

"我去年开始学英语，
今年、明年还要学。"
奶奶说。

Let's think

1 Discuss the Chinese New Year elements in the story with your friend.

2 What else do people do at Chinese New Year? Look at the pictures and tick the correct ones.

New words

1 Learn the new words.

新年

给

多少？

问

这里

糖果

学

今天

| 2026 | 2027 | 2028 | 2029 |

去年　今年　明年

2 Complete the sentences. Write the letters.

a 这里　b 新年　c 给　d 糖果

新年快乐！

____快乐！

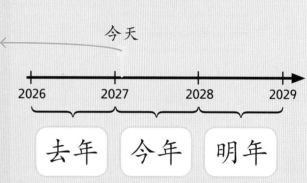

____有红色的____吗？

有。____你。

听听说说 Listen and say

 **1** Listen and match the balls to the correct goals.

2 Look at the pictures. Listen to the st...

1

| 新年 | 今年 |

2

| 多少 | 几 |

3

| 苹果 | 糖果 |

你们喜欢吃水果吗？

喜欢！

④

这里有多少颗糖果？

十五颗。给你一颗。

3 **Look at the questions and pictures. Role-play with your friend.**

1 What colour were the leaves last year?

去年十一月，
我是……的。

2 What colour are the leaves this year?

……四月，
……

3 What will Grandma learn next year?

我……
学……

Task

What do you and your family do on New Year's Day? Talk about it with your friend.

这里是我家。

这是爸爸、妈妈、爷爷、奶奶和我。

我们吃水果。

我们说："新年快乐！"

Paste your photo here.

Game

Listen to your teacher and colour the firecrackers red.

鱼 ( )	糖果 ( )	橡皮 ( )	爸爸 ( )
弟弟 ( )	狗 ( )	姐姐 ( )	看书 ( )
新年 ( )	我 ( )	她 ( )	蛋糕 ( )
多少 ( )	给 ( )	嘴巴 ( )	他 ( )
快乐 ( )	奶奶 ( )	妈妈 ( )	生日 ( )
你 ( )	铅笔 ( )	今年 ( )	上面 ( )

Song

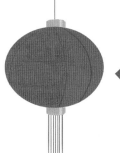

 **05** Listen and sing.

我祝你们新年快乐！
我祝你们新年快乐！
我祝你们今年快乐，
每天都快乐！

课堂用语 Classroom language

带回学校。
Bring it to school.

带回家。
Bring it home.

收好东西。
Put your things away.

15

1 Learn the components. Trace 木 and 忄 to complete the characters.

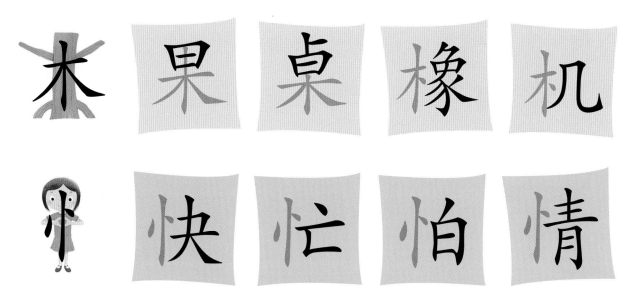

木　果　桌　橡　机

忄　快　忙　怕　情

2 Colour the leaves with the component 木 green and the ones with 忄 red.

朵　汁　快　打　慢　机　李　冷　作　坚　橡　糖

3 Trace and write the characters.

丶 冂 冂 日 旦 旦 早 里 果

丶 丶 忄 忄 忄 快 快

4 Write and say.

新年 ☐ 乐！

给你糖 ☐ 。

汉字小常识 **Did you know?**

Colour the component that encloses another component red.

Some characters include a component which encloses another component on three sides — left, right and bottom.

Cultures

1 Learn about some Chinese New Year traditions.

新年快乐!

People place the red couplets on the doors to express their good wishes for a new year.

The elders in the family usually give red packets to the children. These represent good luck.

People serve their guests 'lucky' snacks in a red container.

2 What do the snacks and sweets symbolize? Write the letters.

a good fortune   b happy life   c sweet life

新年糖果
真好吃。

1 Chinese people like putting paper decorations on windows at Chinese New Year. Make a window decoration.

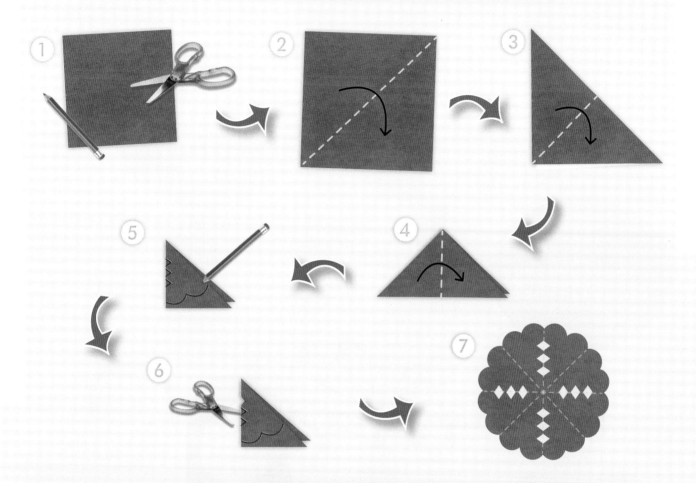

2 Design your own decorations. Paste them on the windows!

新年快乐！

温习 Checkpoint

1 Solve the riddles on the lanterns.

去年我___岁
今年我___岁
明年我___岁

If you want water, you can say ...
请___我水。

Say the year before 今年 in Chinese.

How do you say 'ask' in Chinese?

这里有多少个 ●?
Count and answer in Chinese.

新年快乐!

Say 'I like learning Chinese.' in Chinese.

果

2 Work with your friend. Colour the stars and the chillies.

Words and sentences	说	读	写
新年	☆	☆	🌶
这里	☆	☆	🌶
多少	☆	☆	🌶
糖果	☆	☆	🌶
问	☆	☆	🌶
给	☆	☆	🌶
今年	☆	☆	🌶
去年	☆	🌶	🌶
明年	☆	🌶	🌶
学	☆	🌶	🌶
新年快乐！	☆	☆	🌶
这里有多少颗糖果？	☆	🌶	🌶

Greet people at Chinese New Year	☆

3 What does your teacher say?

21

分享 Sharing

Words I remember

新年	xīn nián	new year
这里	zhè lǐ	here
多少	duō shǎo	how many, how much
糖果	táng guǒ	sweet
问	wèn	to ask
给	gěi	to give
今年	jīn nián	this year
去年	qù nián	last year
明年	míng nián	next year
学	xué	to learn

Other words

身体	shēn tǐ	body
健康	jiàn kāng	healthy
和	hé	and
猜	cāi	to guess
颗	kē	(measure word)
您	nín	you (polite form)
惊喜地	jīng xǐ de	in surprise
开始	kāi shǐ	to begin
还	hái	also
要	yào	to want

OXFORD
UNIVERSITY PRESS

Oxford University Press is a department of the University of Oxford.
It furthers the University's objective of excellence in research, scholarship,
and education by publishing worldwide. Oxford is a registered trade mark of
Oxford University Press in the UK and in certain other countries

Published in Hong Kong by
Oxford University Press (China) Limited
39th Floor, One Kowloon, 1 Wang Yuen Street, Kowloon Bay,
Hong Kong

© Oxford University Press (China) Limited 2017

The moral rights of the author have been asserted

First Edition published in 2017

All rights reserved. No part of this publication may be reproduced, stored in a
retrieval system, or transmitted, in any form or by any means, without the prior
permission in writing of Oxford University Press (China) Limited, or as expressly
permitted by law, by licence, or under terms agreed with the appropriate
reprographics rights organization. Enquiries concerning reproduction outside
the scope of the above should be sent to the Rights Department, Oxford
University Press (China) Limited, at the address above

You must not circulate this work in any other form
and you must impose this same condition on any acquirer

Illustrated by Anne Lee, KK Ng, KY Chan and Wildman

Photographs for reproduction permitted by Dreamstime.com

China National Publications Import & Export (Group) Corporation is an authorized distributor of
Oxford Elementary Chinese.

Please contact content@cnpiec.com.cn or 86-10-65856782

ISBN: 978-0-19-082197-5

10 9 8 7 6 5 4 3 2